ENEMY PLAYBOOK

Powerful New Strategies Demonstrated
By Skeptics to Raise Doubts in Christians

Pastor Lucky

The information provided within this book is for general informational purposes only. The ideas and methods described within this book are the author's personal thoughts.

First Printing Edition: 2022.

Publisher Name: Goof-X LLC

www.pastorlucky.com

ISBN: 979-8-218-01030-0

Library of Congress Number: 2022911802

Things Said About *Enemy Playbook*

"*Enemy Playbook* is so creative and beyond clever. Pastor Lucky managed to use psychology to create schemas that will impact Christian/skeptic debates from this day forward."

–Ralph W. Hood, Jr. PhD
Department of Psychology & UT Alumni Association
Author of *The Psychology of Religion: An Empirical Approach*

"*Enemy Playbook* is cleverly constructed and thoughtful. The scenes are provocative and will inspire deep thought."

–Jacqueline D. Woolley, PhD
Department of Psychology, The University of Texas at Austin

"*Enemy Playbook* has changed the game. Having analyzed the tactics that apologists employ, Lucky found a work-around to utilize both visual and street epistemology style questions to break the scripture's defensive spells. Quickly getting to the heart of the matter, this book is a must for anyone seeking to engage thoughtfully in philosophical debates and tackles the tough subjects with ease."

–Deborah Grace
Author of Crucifying the Bible: Using the Bible to Disprove the Bible

"This book provides an unconventional yet genius approach to debating Christians, which includes both logic and empathy, the latter being very rare in books criticizing religious perspectives."

–Irtza Ali Soomro
Debate and Public Speaking Coach,
International Islamic University Malaysia

"Enemy Playbook aims to teach the reader multiple strategies and tactics for opening minds and liberating intelligent people from irrational and limiting systems of thought."

–Edward L. Zuckerman, PhD
Clinical Psychologist & Author of Clinician's Thesaurus

"A user-friendly and clever book designed to help people understand major flaws in Christianity."

–Jayson X
Author of Bible Problems

To my wife, who is the most consequential

Preface

I wrote this book because of the widespread misunderstanding about the likelihood of the Christian God as the creator of the universe and the source of morality.

The world is filled with the unthinkable, unnecessary suffering of innocent individuals and other creatures. This version of life on Earth and in the universe could have, and would have, been avoided by a God who is loving, omniscient, and omnipotent, no matter how mysteriously he/she/they may work.[1]

The Bible contains many contradictions, dated morals, and other problems.[2] There is, at best, insufficient evidence that the Bible is anything more than a mere collection of writings by people in ancient times, irrespective of how passionately some feel about it.

The same phenomenon that occurs in Christianity and the Bible, occurs in other religions and their sacred texts, before and since the lore of Jesus began.[3] The feeling of true faith and connection to God that Christians experience is the same thing people of other faiths feel. Christians cannot appreciate this significance.

Christianity and the Bible call for the eternal exile and torture of souls, many of whom suffer this fate from the innocent mistake of choosing the wrong God to recognize but worship them, nonetheless.[4]

Objectively, it is far more likely that the universe exists because of one or a combination of: 1) a God who is not loving created it, 2) a God who is not all-knowing created it, 3) a God who is not all-powerful created it, 4) for no reason at all, having no meaning, and 5) some kind of advanced simulation.[5]

No person has a good reason to claim knowledge about the origin of the universe. Yet Christians, because of faith, are certain about their convictions. I hope this book, in some small way, will bring rationality to this topic wherever it leads.

Acknowledgements

Before publishing this book, I wanted to receive tough assessments—feedback from those who are well studied in these areas. I reached out to experts in philosophy, psychology of religion, anthropology, cognitive psychology, and debating.

I received the help I wanted and the inspiration I needed. This book is better for it. I can't tell you how appreciative and humbled I am for the encouragement, generosity and expertise provided to me during this journey. For this, I am grateful to the following individuals:

Julie Exline, PhD; Deborah Grace; Sheldon Helms, PhD; Ralph W. Hood Jr., PhD; Caleb Lack, PhD; Michael Nielsen, PhD; Graham Oppy, PhD; Marc-Henri Sandoz Paradella; Thomas Plante, PhD; Irtza Ali Soomro; Phillips Stevens Jr., PhD; Fabian Suchanek, PhD; Michael J. Telch, PhD; Jacqueline D. Wooley, PhD; Jayson X; and Edward L. Zuckerman, PhD.

Let me also thank the Christians who I interviewed as part of the research for *Enemy Playbook*.

My wife, Kacey, and our sons, Greer and Grant, encouraged me—and cut me slack—so I could focus and finish it. Thanks to them and to our wonderful dogs, the book is done. Thanks to you all!

Contents

Introduction

Enemy Playbook! Seriously? This is the title of the book describing itself as a "fresh and uniquely well-articulated perspective on Christian skepticism"?

The title isn't nearly as colorful as how the book came to be.

As I sought reviews for this book, it had a plain title. Mostly, I sent out copies of the book digitally, but there were *three* hard copies of the manuscript printed. As word spread among churches and religious groups, I was unprepared for the reactions it caused.

Like God himself, I was a first-time author just hoping my book would find an audience. I had plenty of people read it, and some eye-opening messages started coming my way. As I prepared to mail the physical copies, the manuscripts disappeared—all three of them. The rest of the story will be told at a later time.

The experience reminded me of NFL coach Bill Belichick, who once went to questionable lengths to obtain the *other team's plays*—it was that important. He had to know what the strategies of the opposition, or enemy, were.[6] Seeing how coveted the book became, *Enemy Playbook* seemed a fitting title.

These are bold ideas I'm putting forth and I expect them to continue spreading. I would be remiss if I didn't lay bare the complete exposition of what *Enemy Playbook* really is.

I'm about to uncover fascinating machinations of the Christian mind in the "Opening" for you, then reveal "The Strategies" that underpin the book, followed by the real action, the "Scenes," which embody everything taught up to that point.

As you turn the last page, you will have a firm grasp of the techniques that skeptics are already employing on debate stages, in YouTube discussions, at youth groups, and elsewhere. Christians must prepare their defenses as much as skeptics should refine their use of what this book divulges. Brace yourself for *Enemy Playbook*.

Opening

About the Book

What is the right path for you through *Enemy Playbook*?

- If you want to learn how Christians struggle with objectivity, read "The Problem" section.

- If you want to know what makes the scenes in this book effective and how to make your own, go to "Strategies."

- If you want to get straight to the action, go to "Scenes."

Enemy Playbook provides strategies and techniques that skeptics should use in debates with Christians.

You can read *Enemy Playbook* like a guidebook, but it's more than that. It can become part of the interaction, like a game board. The scenes are newfangled ways for a skeptic and Christian to have fruitful discussions and remain on topic.

This book is for anyone who wants to introduce objectivity into their discussions about the trueness of Christianity. Christians, skeptics, and all such debaters should know about the ideas in *Enemy Playbook*. I wrote the "Opening", through to "The Strategies" sections, for skeptics, although I hope it's interesting to anyone. I encourage Christians to read it all, especially the "Scenes."

The Book Is the Beginning

This book lays out the case and provides the strategies and scenes. In addition, I interviewed ten Christians as part of the research for this book. They helped inform, refine, and ultimately support the assertions made in the book. It also showed the effectiveness of some strategies and scenes.

Interviewees provide quantitative feedback about how thought-provoking and doubt-inducing the topics were. The data is being recorded and I will share it on an ongoing basis. You can find them on my website. I refer to these interviews in several places in the book.

Science of Deconstruction

Enemy Playbook is my small contribution to Christian faith deconstruction. Faith deconstruction is the act of analyzing all the aspects of the faith for trueness and utility in pieces.[7] Efforts in neuroscience, psychology, and philosophy are making inroads into this exciting area. Hopefully, a proper discipline will form around deconstruction. I envision machine learning playing a role as well. Perhaps an algorithm will exist one day, which can help anyone employ objectivity and thoughtful analysis when asking the deep questions about our existence through the lens of this and other faiths.

A Note on Atheism

Enemy Playbook is not about atheism. In my opinion, the issue of God being real and believable is altogether different from whether Christianity holds up to scrutiny. This book deals with the latter.

A Message to Brave Christian Readers

Some of what you will read in this book will be offensive to you, or will sound condescending and may appear unfeeling. This is not my intention. I hope you read this to the end, consider it seriously, then arrive at your conclusions about it.

On Empathy

We get why the Christian belief set is so enticing—it's a salve for loneliness, death fears, loss fears, a sense of irrelevance and so forth. For all its shortcomings, Christianity is a Swiss Army knife for all things spiritual that humans care about. For reasons I cannot explain, some of us—Christians for sure—are more affected by the trauma of knowing how fleeting the human experience is and that we may be largely inconsequential other than to ourselves and those who know and love us. Something in the Christian psyche seems to protect them from these harsh concerns as godly faith, which can be very hard for them to relinquish.

Throughout this book, I'll remind you to consider the perspective of Christians respectfully, to take on those views as best you can, and to value attempts by Christians to answer existential questions.

The Problem

About Beliefs

Before we get into the techniques and how to use them, it's good to consider why there's a need for them. This chapter will give you a grasp of the general Christian mindset and go into the various kinds of Christians just enough to decide who and how to debate most effectively.

In this context, let's think about how our belief engine works, how it can go awry, and what happens when it does.

In our daily life, we form beliefs, something challenges them, and they can change the same day.[8] For example, a friend who offers reliable advice suggests that you try "the best restaurant." *This restaurant is the best*. When you go, you quickly decide that it's not what you hoped for. That belief started with your assumption that the restaurant was *the best*. Your dining experience challenged that belief, and it failed the test. You might visit the restaurant again and update that belief. Until then, *this restaurant is not the best*. You see how unstable a belief like this is? It's always resting on the foundation of the next test and a failed test can cause a quick and significant change in the belief.[9] Repeated, similar experiences at the restaurant would cause some stabilization in the belief and it might take more than one experience to update it at that point.

Regardless, such beliefs float on a surface of proof. When the proof evaporates, the belief loses its foundation for existing.

Many of our beliefs work like this, undergoing an ongoing evolution as events occur. This makes sense, right? Hold on to a belief only until it passes the next test, otherwise update it. Recent experiences are the currency of this system.

But the formation and stability of other beliefs isn't so clear. Consider someone who develops a phobia, a belief about a perceived threat from, let's say, public speaking or spiders.[10] Such fears can be hard to rid oneself of, even if the specific phobia's cause isn't obvious. Putting aside why this happens to some but not others, cognitive behavioral therapy (CBT) is a methodology used to treat such fears.[11] For our purposes, it works by exposing the fearful person to *tests*—challenges that force the belief-forming part of the mind to take notice. For example, someone might have harmless spiders get closer and eventually crawl on them. Whatever governs that person's beliefs about spiders, it has little choice but to revise itself incrementally after no problems occur with each new spider interaction. The spider-danger test fails, so fear wanes as the inducement and anxiety response are unpaired.[11]

Some beliefs take hold, hard, seeming to lack a logical basis for forming in the first place. But, when done right, testing of the premise can impact even deep-seated beliefs.[12]

The Christian Framework

Beliefs that are stubbornly stable, like phobias, require effort, focus, repetition, and bravery to update them. If fears like those form a stronghold on beliefs, the Christian paradigm is a stranglehold. In the pages ahead, I'll explain why this is so and the ways it manifests in Christians of varying levels of committedness.

People with a serious phobia typically know they have it and they understand the fear is irrational.[13] They have the perspective of seeing themselves affected by it, and they can imagine being beyond its influence.

This isn't the case with Christians and their beliefs about divinity. Believers are unaware of a particular influence that is in effect.[14] The effect is that a subset of their beliefs is insulated from uncertainty. If uncertainty about Jesus and the Bible is out of the question, then they will never test those ideas. When they suspend testing their beliefs, the belief set becomes isolated from deliberation.

Most Christians will earnestly attempt to consider skeptical arguments. However, a challenge to the faith—placing the belief at risk to revision—somehow cannot occur.[15] This, it seems, is why logic alone is ineffective in persuading a devout Christian to update his, her, or their mind about their faith. A good example of this is how Christians often respond to the question, "Why doesn't God reveal himself now?" Answers you might hear are: 1) you need faith to appreciate it, 2) God wants to see faith exhibited in people, 3) he does reveal himself and 4) a skeptic wouldn't accept it, anyway. A Christian with basic Biblical knowledge, whose belief-testing system is working, would think *God performed many miracles in front of lots of people over hundreds of years, so he could do it now. That's a good question*. But this doesn't happen. Instead of all but ruling out numbers 1 and 2, it leaves Christians to field the question in ways that avoid testing these faith-based beliefs.

It's not enough to think of Christianity as mere superstition. We often use that label pejoratively to describe religious devotion. Recent research into magical thinking and superstitions shows most who embrace such illusory ideas can recognize the irrationality of their thinking, even if they choose to act on it, anyway. This phenomenon, called acquiescence,[16] appears to be absent in Christians' spiritual faith domain—an important distinction.

Unlike our arachnophobic friend from before and his avoidant behaviors, or a baseball fan who rubs a lamp for an hour before a game, many Christians don't seem to recognize the corruption in their judgment. They believe the act of defending Christianity, despite scant evidence for it, is valid and rational. We can say *scant* because there's no categorically unique evidence for Christianity. The body of evidence Christians cite is indistinguishable from the type of support many non-Christian theists confirm their faiths with, including: a transcendent prophet, afterlife claims, unfalsifiable predictions, "miracles" testified to by acolytes, a self-evident holy book, and so forth.

As part of the research for this book, I asked ten Christians if they understood how alike their faith experiences were to people of other religions. They could see similarities, but ultimately, they all felt there were intangibles that made their Christian experiences special compared to those of other faiths. The kinds of reasons given were typical and, in my view, uncompelling: quoting of the Bible; there is only one true God, the Christian God; others may pray, but they're not hearing God; etc.

Subconscious Refusal

What's going on with this powerful protection of a belief set in the mind of the Christian? Actually, the normal belief-forming process is alive and well in Christians, just not in this one domain. There's a subconscious refusal to let uncertainty touch this belief set.

Now, the term *refusal* implies a decision is being made. Can Christians *subconsciously* refuse to consider ideas that threaten the faith? When the believer makes relevant assumptions without acknowledging them, an implicit bias, or subconscious refusal, is in effect.[17]

During my interviews with Christians, refusal was apparent when I asked two of them if there were any wrongdoings in the following two cases. I wanted to see if they would apply the same standard to what is essentially the same dilemma.

> *#1. At the outset of a business trip, a company assigns two bosses to an employee. Each boss gives her a task, which contradicts the other's task. The tasks are due before the right supervisor can be identified. She does the task assigned by the first boss.*

> *#2. A follower of Islam on their first trip to a western country learns about Christianity, the*

Bible, and the revelation. The faiths have competing demands with no apparent way to resolve them. The person remains Muslim.

The interviewees said the employee made no wrongdoing in scenario #1 and that no punishment was due. However, they said a wrongdoing occurred in the second case and that it warranted a punishment by God. In other words, the Christians refused to acknowledge that, like in the business trip case, there was no obvious way for the Muslim to resolve the issue, and that God imposing a negative consequence for a wrong guess would be pointless, and even counterproductive.

The following is a visualization of the Christian mind's rejection of uncertainty and belief testing. In Figure 1, the orb represents a subconscious refusal to accept threats to that framework. Willingness, represented by the cube, is eclipsed by the refusal.[18]

Figure 1

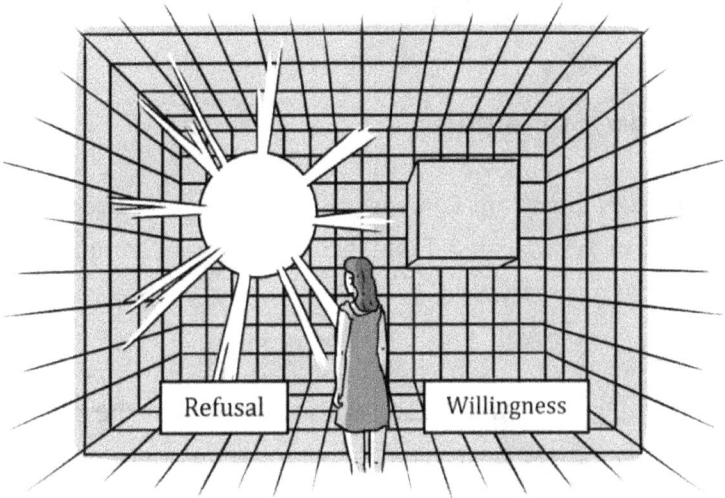

To watch a devout Christian debate Christianity with a skeptic is to see the refusal in action. It can be both vexing and fascinating to watch a Christian have his reasoning invalidated and then defend the belief with a second, less-sound rationale, as if the deflection of the faith test had not just occurred.

To a lesser extent, this subconscious refusal occurs in everyone.[19] If you received some terrible, but trustworthy news about someone you love, you might, for a brief time, refuse to accept it—it's just too much. This is similar to what I think the Christian is doing when they invalidate information which threatens what will not be threatened, what cannot be: their faith.

Evidence Starvation

Refusal by Christians to consider worldly alternatives in this domain shows itself interestingly through something I call *evidence starvation*.

Christians have certainty about beliefs which have weak foundations. The mind detects this condition. When beliefs like these become strong enough, without enough supporting evidence for them, it causes a state of evidence starvation. In this state, things that may not be evidence of anything other than their own existence appear to be the proof the believer is craving. The evidence-starved Christian sees beauty in nature, kindness shown, and wishes coming true as signs of God's grace. The mind does what it must to fill the void, so it attaches the best candidates for foundations it can find to those beliefs.

This tendency is known as misattribution.[20] However, when certainty itself is believed to cause the perceived effect, it's evidence starvation. To clarify, Christians say that only good people go to heaven, but God won't allow you in unless you have certainty about Christianity. You can pray that a wish will be granted, but God won't answer it without true faith. You can go to church to experience the holy spirit, but it won't happen without conviction for Jesus and Christianity.

Figure 2

Evidence Starvation

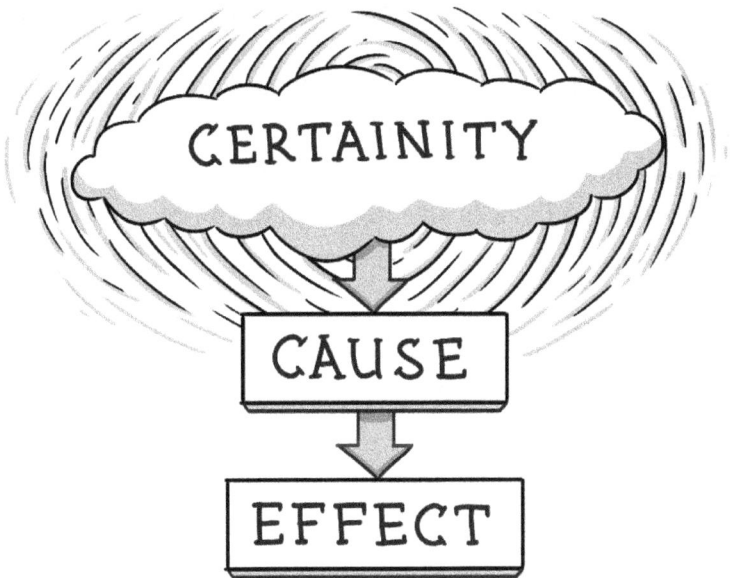

The Closed Loop of Christian Certainty

These issues with Christian faith manifest a vicious cycle in reasoning.[21] Whether the believer is casual or extreme in their views, it ultimately leads to the same phenomenon, where the belief feeds the basis of the belief and vice versa.

We can see the closed loop effect in Christian literalists at every level: the Bible as history, the harsh fate awaiting the unrepentant, and so forth. Moderate Christians will, however, accept some contradictions. So, we must ask deeper, more central questions of less-extreme believers.

In Figure 3, for example, you can see how the fundamentalist Christian thinks. He starts and ends with the assumption of biblical divinity. You cannot ask about problems with the Bible because there can't be problems with the Bible. You cannot compare their faith with Islam, for example, because the Bible doesn't recognize Muhammad as a prophet.[22] You cannot ask whether God's action is moral or not because there's no way it couldn't be.[23]

Figure 3

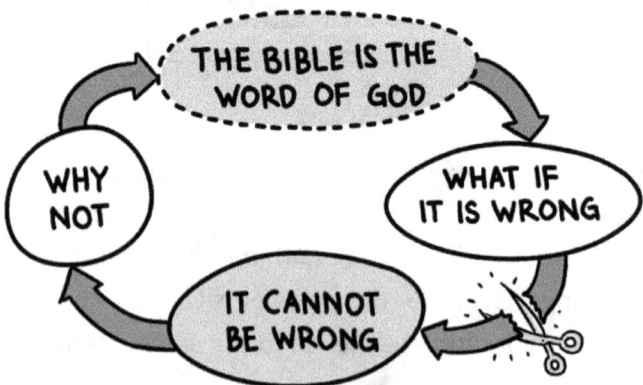

In this example of closed-looped thinking where the Christian, against all hopes, questions his opinions, the weak point is the assumption that the Bible must be true. In the "Scenes" and "Strategies" sections, you'll learn ways to make inroads to fallacies like these.

The Requirements

There is a set of underlying requirements that Christians have of their faith. It's useful to be aware of these needs when making your case and building new scenes. Let me convey them in terms of a function, which takes an input, does something with it, then provides an output. Figure 4 illustrates the Christian Faith Function. It's what a Christian must start and end with in exchange for their dedication to the faith.

Figure 4

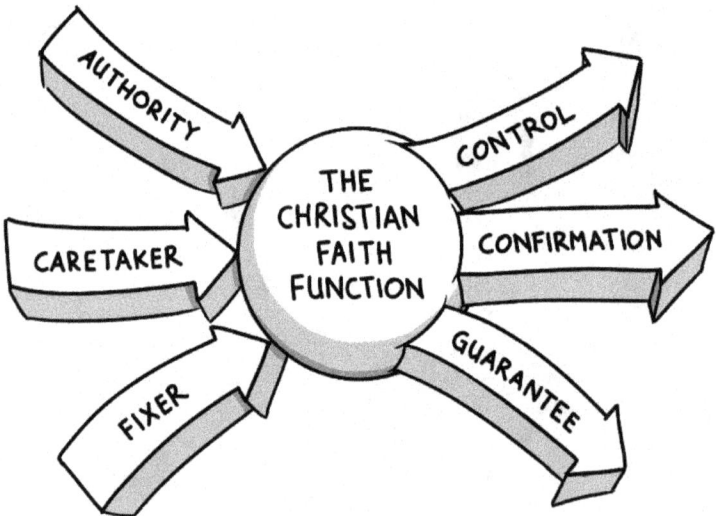

The Inputs

Christians require more structure than what the world offers, and Christianity is the framework that delivers on those needs. These inputs are the pre-requirements.

Authority. The faithful Christians demand an ultimate authority, someone who is responsible for their existence, who makes a set of rules and explanations, and who places expectations on them. To them, God is this authority, and he is real, unchallenged, and unchanging. It's too important not to be.

Caretaker. It's a neat idea to imagine having a cosmic partner, a caretaker, who is always there, who keeps you company, and provides help and advice in the most personal ways. When you witness Christians' refusal to allow the faith test, a big part of this is the denial that their spiritual custodian isn't real.

Fixer. Inconceivable to Christians is the notion that spiritual justice might not ultimately prevail. It's too alluring for them not to fantasize that everything that should matter will matter in the end. This idea of a fixer, a master untangler of all that needs sorting out, is yet another reason the willingness valve remains closed on ideas that would expose the faith to challenge.

The Outputs

The concept of a supportive enforcer works only if there are certain assurances given. Christians must believe the administrator will reliably bring order to their earthly and spiritual lives. The outputs represent these assurances.

Control. The revelation provides a story and structure for God and morality, but Christians need order for their own lives. By embracing the Bible, and committing to the faith, they take the action to participate in a structure that offers reign over their fate and others. Christians need to affect outcomes that would otherwise be beyond their influence.

Confirmation. Christians employ a convenient method for dealing with all the religions competing for our faith: form unassailable certainty around the one that feels right to them. One of the many upsides to Christian faith is "knowing" you're right, that you chose the right faith. There's a calming resonance every Christian enjoys in exchange for refusing to treat faith like any other rationale.

Guarantee. Say what you will about the Bible. It gives the believer a sense that it means what it says. The rules are tough, and the consequences are harsh, but the message is clear: devotion to God will provide the outcome the Christian wants. Christians wonder if they're going to live up to the heaven-bound standard, but they're sure that God delivers on righteousness. There's a bona fide quality to the Bible itself and the legend of Christianity. Christians believe they've bought into something embodying legitimacy, which has the reliability of a meaningful guarantee.

Bear in mind, most of these requirements are things that non-Christians also crave. Who wouldn't want a force that will rectify injustices? Who doesn't appreciate assurances that if they follow through, others will, too?

The Christian simply takes the added step of insisting that these things are the function of an omnipotent authority. As you continue through this book, be mindful that having these needs is reasonable. We all have a sense that an ultimate fairness should somehow affect the human existence. Christians can't help but demand that it be so. Be empathetic of their requirements and how irrepressible such tendencies are for them. Demonstrating that you understand these things will positively affect debate outcomes for you, the skeptic, and your debate opponents will welcome it.

Pastor Lucky

The Solution

Changing the Debate

In this book, what we care about is encouraging objectivity. We want to speak to Christians about the problems, contradictions, and fallacies of their faith and for them to understand, even if, for whatever reason, they want to retain their faith. But let's be clear: the very best defenses for Christianity are based on poor reasoning, wishful thinking, or both.[24]

This is true for confirmation biases toward historical evidence. Christians accept, on face, dubious and inconsistent accounts of Jesus' supposed resurrection by a handful of witnesses. Why not, then, hold sacred the Buddha's magical competitions, confirmed by hundreds,[25] or the water flowing from the hands of Muhammad, which was not only seen but drunk by over one thousand men?[26] The answer is confirmation bias—Christians affirm that which they want to be true and ignore or invalidate claims that could diminish their faith.

Such fallacious reasoning extends to ontological and epistemic arguments.[27, 28] A notable example is Descartes' argument for the proof of God in *Discourse on the Method*.[29] Even if one were to accept its premise, there is not a word in it that points to the Christian God or the veracity of the Bible. Yet Christians use it, and abstract theories like it, as added support for the truth of Christianity. Unfounded wishes are how Christians get from "I think therefore I am" to "Jesus is the son of God."

Insistence of such poorly substantiated assertions forms a stifling effect on communication and openness to ideas in debates about Christian skepticism.

Moreover, the refusal Christians bring to discussions with skeptics prevents these talks from qualifying as debates. In philosophical debates, something compelling said by one side should matter to the other.[30] Oftentimes, this isn't the case for Christians. They may tell you this explicitly: "nothing will change my mind!" Even educated, well-meaning Christians attending debates are ultimately working to evade objectively sound reasoning. If they weren't, then one of them would've accurately answered the following question by now: what can you objectively claim about the origin of the universe on behalf of Christianity, that Muslims, Jews, and Hindus can't claim on behalf of their faiths?

The Christian-based debate stalemate is a central problem that this book will help to counteract.

What we want for effective communication in debate, as well as for the well-being of Christians, is to squelch the refusal and amplify the willingness. Only after we've achieved this can belief-testing resume. If it does, then objectivity can begin to govern this belief set, like it does many of the Christian's other beliefs. Figure 1 represents the dominance of refusal in the steady-state Christian's faith, whereas Figure 5 shows the intended state, in which willingness exposes the beliefs to uncertainty. Achieving this state will require overwhelming emphasis to be placed on the willingness, which is a primary challenge for the skeptic to elicit.

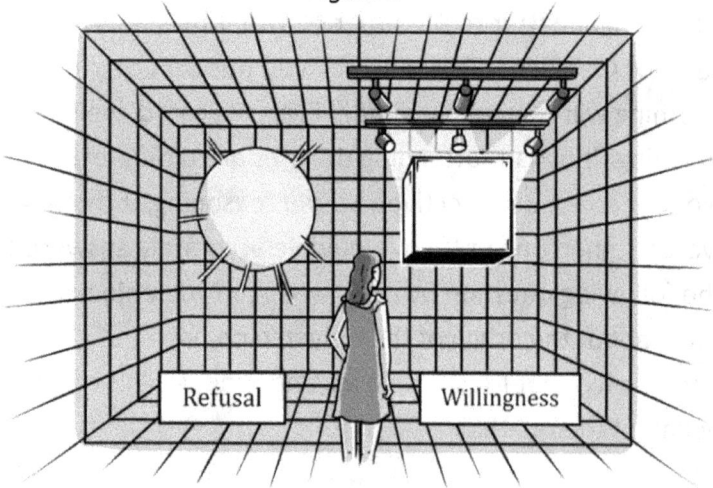

Figure 5

The Christian needs enough willingness to consider news that threatens the Christian framework, allows challenges to it, and provides an opportunity to affect the belief set.

The Way Around Logic

So far, I've made the case that, in this domain, Christians are resistant to persuasion by logic and that it's because of a subconscious refusal to permit intermingling of faith-based beliefs and challenges to them.

So, what effective strategy am I suggesting instead of logic? How do you make inroads to things like closed-loop thinking and evidence starvation? What hope is there of creating doubt in a Christian about their faith, given those needs are being met by said faith?

Think of the problem of Christian intransigence—the refusal—as a ball of string with tight knots in it. It isn't so much of a complicated problem to straighten the string as it is time-consuming and tedious to nudge each knot loose, one at a time.

We can find and amplify the elusive willingness by approaching the fallacies from a wide range of perspectives. You will respond to brief moments of willingness with effective belief-testing in a way that demonstrates genuine empathy for the Christian. You aren't solving a problem of forcing logic and reason to work at once. You are slowly teasing out the willingness to consider your good arguments. You are strategically showcasing your flexible perspective for your opponent so they may emulate it.

The strategies work by giving you new ways of loosening those proverbial knots and interacting with your Christian debate partners in ways that subtly reduce the refusal.

About the Scenes

Practically speaking, the scene is our solution. It's the primary means for bringing about these important changes.

In this book, a scene is a carefully planned story idea. The scene calls into question assumptions or assertions about Christianity in a hypothetical scenario. It serves to advance the debate beyond the typical stalemates.

Scenes should include an image that sets the context and reinforces the story, accompanied by a set of thought-provoking questions.

Scenes can be based on analogies, symbolism, thought experiments, or any construct that raises questions about the presumptions about Christianity's trueness.

Above all, a scene provides a conversational framework for belief testing. It's a context to help articulate a Christian idea or assumption, then test that idea in a way that illustrates its fallacies and shortcomings.

You will find twenty scenes in this book. You can create your own when you understand the ideas of the following section, "The Strategies."

Pastor Lucky

The Strategies

Strategies Summary

This section provides the underlying methods for creating effective scenes and shows you why they work. It also gives you the tools to create your own scenes. You don't need this information in order to make use of the existing scenes, however. You can get started using them right now.

Using these strategies, and combining them to make scenes, will provide a good basis for a debate or discussion, and will expand the opportunities for objectivity to play a bigger role in that discussion overall.

You want to create thought-provoking scenes, but that's not the end of the conversation. You must be able to defend your positions with grace and respect. *Enemy Playbook*'s strategies include discussion skills and tips that start before, and continue after, you've introduced the scenes.

Why Use Them?

The strategies help create a clear, complete, and useful scene that gives definition and constraints to a debate. The strategies amplify your sound reasoning and valid arguments. You are half a debate. Be the better half. Make effective arguments, yes, but use the unique and finesse-based approach this book offers to ensure your debate extends beyond others' stalemates.

Breaking the is-because-it-is cycle and overshadowing the Christian's subconscious refusal by drawing out objectivity are what you're after. If these happen, progress gets made. These strategies will help you achieve those goals.

Strategies

Know the Nature of the Discussion

We use the first strategy before delving into the scenes themselves. It's about the nature of the discussion itself.

What tends to occur when a Christian and a skeptic discuss faith is that the Christian, unbeknownst to them, suspends their standards for applying logic throughout a discussion to keep their responses aligned with the faith. Protecting the faith will, unfortunately, trump the concession of the good points you make.

Respectfully remind the Christian about this if need be. Be sincerely willing to have a superficial, non-analytical chat about their faith if that's all they're willing, or able, to do. However, if a *debate* occurs, then a standard should exist in the Christian's mind that you're responsible for creating and updating. And you can say that.

You could say to the Christian:

If you say God is fair, and I provide good examples of him being unfair, then you should be willing to update your faith position, even though your overall faith remains intact.

If you say the Bible comes from an omniscient being, and I provide good examples that show the Bible does not appear to be the product of an all-knowing God, then you should be willing to update your faith position even though your overall faith remains intact.

Likewise, if you make the point that I can't know with certainty what God would do, then I should be willing to concede, even though my overall position toward Christianity may not change.

You should add:

If you agree to consider updating your faith position as we talk, it doesn't mean you're relinquishing your overall faith in Christianity. By the same token, I should be able to accept when you point out the limits of my skepticism.

If we both resist matching our responses to our starting positions, we can go beyond the stalemate most debates like this end at. If, in the process, some face is lost to our respective peers in the pursuit of earnest debate, that's probably not a bad thing.

Invalidating the Premise

The goal of the scene is to produce doubt about weak Christian premises. To do this, you should be able to distill a general Christian assertion down to a concise statement, then imagine what would invalidate it. I'm talking about those all-important tests and challenges discussed earlier.

You could start with the general idea that *God answers prayers*. Then, refine the idea to prayers that are made to the right God by true believers and for selfless reasons. Continue focusing on the small scale of a prayer. The final assertion you would test in your scene could be:

> "The Christian God answers good-hearted prayers of devout Christians for little things."

Next, build a scenario that would illustrate a qualifying prayer request being denied. One easily visualized idea is a pastor with a mini beach ball and praying for it to rise a foot into the air. To cover the good-hearted angle, you could add that the church provisionally raised $100,000 for the needy so long as God grants this simple prayer for this worthy Christian at his Sunday service.

As you know, the pastor will fail. God won't grant this devout Christian his good-hearted prayer for a little ball to float for a moment, not even to help those needy folks. By the way, you don't have to state this explicitly. You only have to show the inevitability of what your scene suggests.

Perspective Switching

Being aware of the perspective you set the stage from is helpful, but changing the story angle from first- to second- to third-person and back again is a powerful strategy to counter the perspective paralysis of your Christian opponent. The inability to see faith-based commitments from other viewpoints is part of the Christian tendency. If you can force a change in their viewpoint, you'll have a far more persuadable subject than you would if you allowed them to see the scene from the perspective they want to.

Keep moving the lens so the Christian knows what's really there. One might only ever think the moon is a circle until they see it from another perspective and realize it's actually a sphere. Think of this from the perspective-challenged Christian's standpoint.

Redundant Descriptions

Even when you describe things well, some people will forget details or not register them in the first place. So, repeat a point or refer to it in slightly different ways to help assure your scene lands the same way to you as it does for your listener. Stating the same message two or three times in slight variations helps the ideas penetrate. And the image you use can be one of those ways of amplifying the message in your storyline.

Your listener is unconsciously prioritizing what they'll remember, so help the process along by hedging on your descriptions and restating key ideas where applicable.

Pictures

A good way to create vivid imagery, naturally, is with an actual picture. That's why there's one with nearly every scene in this book. In keeping it simple, start with a blank page and only add in those parts needed to make your point or sell the scene.

The efforts you put into making your imagery strong, simple, and clear will shine light on the edges of your willingness cube, so to speak. We know it's important to compete with the Christian's subconscious refusal to weigh those arguments.

You can make pictures yourself. They need not be perfect works of art. You can also, as I did, find someone skilled at drawing vignettes to make them for you.

A side benefit is that the images will have value beyond the single debate you made them for. You can use your images in videos, for example, to serve as a pretext and backdrop for additional conversations and debates.

Finally, be mindful about the implied tone of a scene's picture. It takes some thought, and maybe a few drafts, to create an image that explicates without being overly satirical or condescending.

Effective Themes

It isn't hard to find problems of validity with the Bible or the foundations of Christianity.[31] I've provided a starter list of such issues here: nonsensical claims and rules, lack of proportional reactions, not exhibiting omniscience, not exhibiting omnipotence, cruelty and depravity, and indifference to misunderstandings, to name a few.

Don't limit yourself to these themes. Creative, thoughtful readers will produce many more than I've listed or embodied in the scenes.

Separate God from Christianity

Christian skepticism is a deep and challenging subject. There's much to know about how Christians think, the Bible, and so forth. We don't always look at it this way, but whether God exists at all is a subject unto itself. What kind of tree is growing in your yard is a different matter altogether from whether there's a tree in your yard at all.

I urge you to apply skepticism to these subjects, one or the other, but don't approach both in the same scene. The prospect of defending two subjects simultaneously should be reason enough for you not to do it. However, there are other reasons to take them on individually.

In the murky domains of religious faith and the origin of the universe, it's easier for your debate partners to avoid answering the hard questions if they're able to move between topics as needed. For example, a stalled debate about whether the book of Genesis is an actual or metaphorical account can subtly turn into one about the need for some creator, regardless of how one interprets that book. The fallacy in this case: if we're debating about *the way* in which to interpret Genesis, then we've quietly established the preceding step—the importance of the book to begin with.

It goes the other way as well. A Christian might refer to the Kalam cosmological argument, a reasonable starting point for a discussion about the origin of the universe.[32] But this assertion gets erroneously used as support for the trueness of Christianity and the Christian God's role in that process. Kalam and similar arguments assert the need for *a* god, but not the Christian one, specifically.

If you want a Christian/skeptic debate to be more productive, then block the connection between the topics of Christianity's trueness and the existence of God. The scene, helped by the use of a picture, will better constrain the discussion.

Asking Impactful Questions

The questions stimulate the discussion past what the scene says. You can use a mix of long and short ones. I use a format that suggests a yes or no type answer, but I do this merely to help organize the answering process. Your opponent may affirm or deny the question, then expand on their reasoning.

I would prepare at least two questions to make the most of a scene opportunity for discussion. I would also refrain from asking more than four or five questions in a scene. You want the discussion to remain interesting, not drag on. You should be able to cover the range of things you want answered with three good questions.

Remember, you can use questions as a way of repeating or reinforcing your narrative.

In the same way that your scene is a test of an assertion, each question can be a test. When in doubt about how to phrase a question, you can always use an if/then format: *if* God hears the thoughts of non-believers, *then* why won't he show it? You get the effect.

Storylines

Put thought into the stories of your scenes. They should be inherently convincing. They should bring together the Christian assertion you spotlight and the test you use to refute it. In many cases, you will use analogies and metaphors as a basis for your story. If yours seems merely satisfactory to you, find a better way of conveying the idea.

Multifaceted Is Better

You should strive to include more than one aspect of skepticism if possible. Examples include prayer, heaven, God's cruelty, and so forth.

Examining one issue can be too theoretical. It provides an unnecessary challenge for the Christian participant to become immersed in the scene. Also, the story of your scenes will probably be more interesting when they mimic real-life complexity, containing more than one matter of consideration.

Combining Strategies

Use multiple strategies in the same scene. The more the better. Unexpectedly changing perspectives, repeating important reminders, painting a clear picture, and so forth will help make your points better, faster, and provide a more lasting impact.

Titles

Each scene has a title, and the title should hint at what the reader can expect. Other than that, I don't think this component of the scene is very important. Keep your title short and descriptive.

Strategies to Avoid

Trickery & Baiting

Do you appreciate being led dishonestly in conversations? Does such a tactic facilitate good communication? No and no. So, for the benefit of the debate, refrain from questions that strawman, gaslight, or otherwise set up the Christian as an exercise to expose them as mere hypocrites. You'll activate the Christian's defenses if you use such disingenuous techniques.

Your number one inner-debate goal should be creating circumstances that tease out the willingness. You want to encourage objectivity with an earnest approach that facilitates such a discussion. Christian opponents won't only have the ability, but the desire to look at the scene from a lens of your choosing, which will lead to the right outcomes, or at least the right outlook.

Christians have some deeper things going on, you know that. In their state, they'll reject competing ideas that threaten the Christian framework. You don't have that excuse! Use strategies to help foster a debate that encourages objectivity in your opponent. Winning points with lame tactics will prove counterproductive.

Magisteria

In the 1990's, biologist Stephen Jay Gould said science and religion are separate domains that should stay out of each other's area—he called it *non-overlapping magisteria*. Christians welcomed it since an Ivy League scientist offered it and it provided cover and legitimacy for faith-based arguments.[33]

In my opinion, you should not subscribe to this idea, not if you want to avoid debate stalemate, which is what this book aims to help you do. If someone believes a supreme being created the universe, they're entitled to that opinion, and no one can prove they're wrong. However, Christians use *reason* to support specific, historic claims of the Bible, then fail to apply that same logic in matters that bring scrutiny of their faith. As Sam Harris has said, Christians like to play tennis without the net.[34]

Don't cede reason to Christians, not even to defend their faith. Dozens of competing faith stories all using the same rationale crowd the domain of religion, which is an enormous problem for religions. Create and use scenes that reference Christianity in the same realm as everything else that's being defended with reason.

Caution If You Steel-Man

When you speculate the opposition's questions aloud, and then argue against those, you are *steel-manning*.[35] This is dangerous to do as Christians have a heightened sense of rebelliousness for having their arguments defined, then invalidated, by others.[36]

You can steel-man earnestly, but to avoid setting off the Christian's alarms, keep the following guideline in mind: don't make someone's argument for them unless you can truly empathize with their viewpoints. To make a steel-man's point, you should almost support that perspective yourself, so you make a case that your opponent and any spectators can respect.

Unsound Arguments

Almost as damaging as deliberate trickery is ignorance. Errors, fallacious arguments, and overly broad claims are all things that warn your opponent that you're unprepared to discuss a topic. Use care to avoid asserting or responding with unsound reasoning. Remember, the take-away message won't be that you made an isolated, good-hearted mistake. It will be that you're inadequate to teach them anything new. It degrades your credibility.

Remember that you have the option of conceding points or admitting you don't know. Doing so isn't only emblematic of a good skeptic, it's strategic because it demonstrates your commitment to honest discourse to your debate partner, which is as important as any points of merit you strive to make.

Some opportunities for avoiding unsound arguments are available only to skeptics. Defense of Christianity ultimately relies on faith in God, which, as stated before, is a rationale used by non-Christians as well. We won't label it as wrong, but we *will* say that faith is an uncompelling basis on which to make cases about matters of reason. Be ready to call into question purely faith-based claims continually for that reason, and you can maintain an advantage if you eschew your own errors and fallacies in reasoning.

Technical Matters

Biblical technical contradictions should matter to Christians, but they typically don't. "Average" Christians will avoid getting bogged down with esoteric scripture. They can dismiss potential problems of the Bible with a range of options such as: it's meant to be interpreted, you're taking it out of context from ancient times, faith isn't like math and it cannot be cornered with reason, etc.

Whereas extreme believers see only perfection in the Bible and therefore balk at all claims to the contrary. Literalists have their own set of Bible defenses including: an all-powerful God could have easily suspended natural rules long ago, if God said it then it must be right, without receiving the gift of faith from God then one cannot understand it's true meaning, and so forth.

In any case, dealing with such technicalities will detract from your efforts and dilute your points. Yes, if you add up even conservative dates of lifetimes from Adam to Abraham based on Genesis 1, 5 & 11, you get an Earth that's approximately 6000 years old, and this isn't the effect of poetic symbolism that some say explains the fancy of some Bible stories.[37] Regardless, you'll find using this kind of argument to achieve your goal of drawing out willingness to test faith beliefs to be ineffective.

Argue against fundamentals, not the incidentals of faith. The best issues to raise in your debates should be the ones that diminish those key requirements mentioned earlier. Is God less of a caretaker to a Christian because you mock Noah's impossibly old age? No. But you can reference the Bible's assertion that a camel gets through a needle's eye easier than a rich man does to heaven, like in Matthew 19:24.[38] This goes to the unattainable standard for entry to heaven, lessening the value of the guarantee, a crucial aspect of the faith.

Tactics

On the subject of using tactics, let me contrast the approach of my book with that of Greg Koukl's *Tactics*. *Tactics* is a useful guide for apologetics or any Christian who simply wants to avoid losing arguments defending Christianity. To me, *Tactics* is a cheat sheet for bullshitting your way to a debate winner's box. Worse though, is that in this book, Koukl acknowledges morally reprehensible aspects of his faith, then dismisses them as distractions from the effectiveness of his tactics. He'd rather he, and his readers, come off looking good, like winners! One notable example is Deepak Chopra's surprisingly good question about non-believers being destined for hell. Koukl remarks, "If I had answered directly—'Yes, people who do not believe just like me are going to hell'—the debate would have been over." Koukl goes on to say: "Chopra's query would have succeeded in painting me with an ugly stereotype."[39] The *Tactics* author models disturbing indifference to God's heinous revenge policy toward non-Christians in favor of pretense and misdirection.

Don't do this. Be forthright in skeptical discussions and disagreements. If you find yourself on shaky ground, acknowledge it and move on. I hope that *Enemy Playbook*, edgy title aside, will have the opposite effect that *Tactics* seems to advocate, which is perception and appearance over substance, not to mention tacit approval of revenge and torture. Please refrain from using cheap tricks and evasion when employing the strategies in this book.

Next Steps

I've discussed how the minds of Christians safeguard their beliefs about God from challenges, what your goals are to make a difference, and how this can affect debates and communications. I then explained the various strategies that underlie effective scenes and discourse. Now, let's move to the scenes themselves, which are what you'll use to frame debates with Christians.

Pastor Lucky

Scenes

A scene contains a description, has an image, and is followed by a set of thought-provoking questions. Use scenes as a context for discussions about Christian assertions.

You'll notice that many of the questions call for a yes or no formatted response. Make opponents aware that you do this merely to give a starting point for replies, not to box them into final, binary answers that you can take out of context. It's important you explain this up front to avoid the backfire effect.[40] A Christian who senses their reasons for believing are under attack will become more rebellious, more committed to the position, and less open to deliberation. You will trigger a defensive posture in your opponent if you fail to prepare for it.

Encourage opponents to expand on their answer and express interest in learning what that detail and context will be. And remind yourselves to avoid attempts to strawman, or otherwise humiliate, debate opponents. It isn't just for honor's sake. If you are winning points by focusing attention on things incidental to your effective points, then you aren't winning on merit. What does that say about the strength of your arguments?

If you've become familiar with the strategies in the last chapter, you have enough effective ways to make your own convincing cases and to thwart the effects of poor reasoning from your opponent.

Cosmic Stop Sign Problem

Let's say there is a tourist attraction on Earth called God's Cosmic Stop Sign. It has been there for as long as anyone can remember.

Everyone knows where it is and can visit it. It is, in most respects, an ordinary stop sign, but unlike any other, it hovers twelve inches above the ground. It is clearly defying the law of gravity. On the sign is a message: "Stop. Be aware of the one true Christian God." Amazingly, the message appears to each person in the language they understand best.

Questions

If God performed many miracles in front of people in biblical times, then wouldn't it make sense for a miracle to exist today that shows the power of the Christian God?

A sign like this means people would need little or no faith to believe in God. This might make it too easy on them, defeating a purpose God wants people to experience. If the sign was there, and the same expectations existed for worshiping God, avoiding sin, repentance, and so forth, would that be a bad thing considering the benefits, like confirming people's hope for God and preventing wars?

Hebrews 11:6 says it's impossible to please God without faith.[41] Even if someone has faith in God, how would they know his identity? What means does God give people to differentiate the true God from the imposter faiths, each having their own sacred text which requires exclusive loyalty?

Don't Forget the Future

Imagine that you are God—the Christian God. You made the universe and now you'll reveal yourself to humanity. You are going to produce the Bible, starting with the Old Testament.

You have great wisdom to share, but you have more than that. You're omniscient, so you know how society will have developed in the twenty-first century just as well as you do life in ancient times. You know everything that took place between those times. None of your words will become dated, as you know everything, about all times.

Questions

You foresee many potential problems with men writing the Bible for you, especially in ancient times. And you can see it will be impossible for people to tell your book apart from other divinely claimed works. As God, will these realizations guide you to solve some of these problems before they occur?

Will you be careful about using violence on others in your stories, given that people will model their behavior after yours as inherently moral?

Will your Bible condone slavery since you know how destructive and hurtful it will be one day?

Can't Choose Problem

Get a sheet of paper, draw a line down the middle. Draw a small circle in the center of the right side.

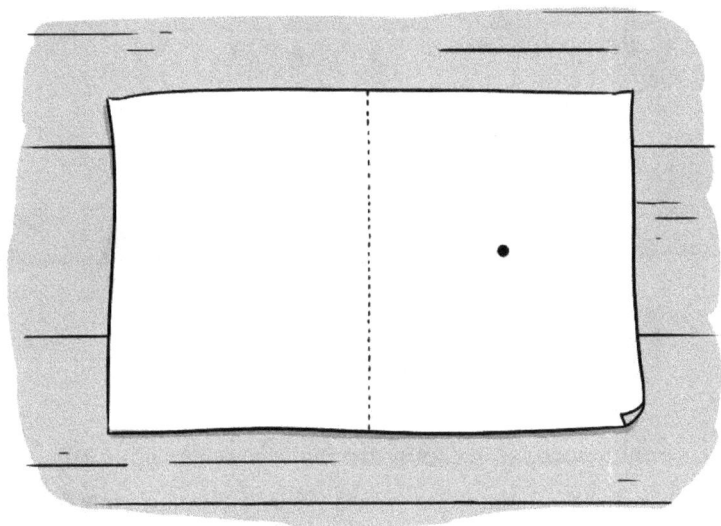

Put your left hand over the blank side. Put your right hand over the mark.

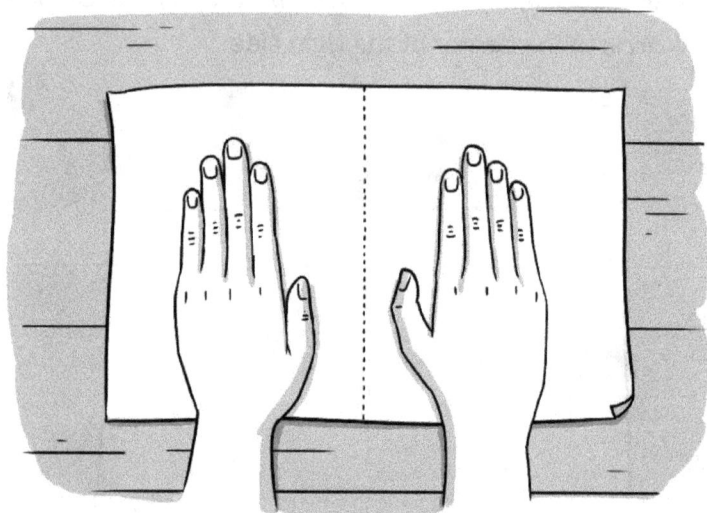

Now, **make yourself believe the mark is under your left hand**. Seriously, for a minute or so, try to change your mind about what you think the truth of the mark's location is.

As you make your attempt, imagine two additional circumstances:

- there is a $1 million prize for switching your belief: right side to left side

- you are connected to an infallible lie detector machine

You are then asked where the mark is.

Questions

Were you ultimately able to force a change in your belief about the location of the mark on the paper?

You just showed how hard it is to lie to yourself about what you believe. Do you think this phenomenon applies to someone who cannot bring themself to believe in Christianity, even if they want to?

Now you understand what it means to want to believe in something you don't believe. Do you have a problem with putting your faith in a God who punishes people for something that isn't really within their power to change?

The Hole I Saved You From

Imagine you took a friend, Joe, on a walk far out in the woods. It's a place he has never been. He's a little nervous, but he figures he has you as a guide.

As you walk together, you tell Joe something startling. In this area, you've built a trap, a hole he will surely fall into and can never escape. But you have good news: if he promises to do as you say, you'll save him from it. Frightened and without other options, Joe agrees to your terms.

Fortunately, Joe did what he had to and made his way home.

Joe tells his wife about the dangerous condition you created and then saved him from. Naturally, your actions appall her. She calls you on the phone and tells you to never contact either of them again.

Now, think about God, who brought you into a world with an eternal lake of fire he created that you will fall into if you don't abide by his rules and worship him (Revelations 19–21).[41] Like you offered Joe on the nature walk, God gives you a way to avoid the terrible fate: pledge yourself to him—or else.

Questions

Was what you did to Joe the kind of thing you do to someone you care about?

Can you see the similarity between the situation you put Joe in and the one God put you in here in this world and in your spiritual life?

For a moment, try to put yourself in Joe's shoes. After the guide's revelation, he reminds you he loves you and that he made a big sacrifice to be on the walk with you. Does this comfort you or justify his actions?

If you wouldn't put someone you care about into this position, why would you defend God for doing virtually the same thing, but with far more serious consequences?

Visiting Alien Problem

Beings from another planet arrive on Earth. Somehow, we can talk with them. They know nothing about religion, but they're interested in the idea.

Leaders of the world's great religions gather to make their cases. They present their holy books and all state why they hold their faith, clarifying that only one can be right.

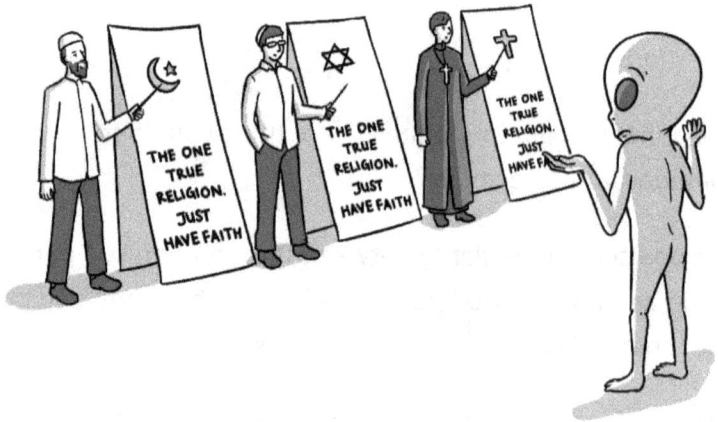

The alien takes a day to review the findings. He finds big faults with all the faiths, starting with lack of reliable evidence. Also, he says the books do not appear to be divinely inspired, and that there is nothing remarkable about these texts except the claims, which must be fictitious, at least for two of them. And any claim made by one faith could easily be made by another—and *is* made by the others.

Each of the leaders then tells the alien he must have faith in order to understand it. The alien asks which one he should have faith in, given that all three are mutually exclusive to one another. The church leaders argue among themselves, unable to resolve the alien's questions.

Questions

Is it a problem for the trueness of Christianity that when an alien gets a fresh look at Earth's religions, he cannot tell whether Christianity is the right faith?

Can you think of anything the Christian leader could have said to the alien that differentiates Christianity as true from the other faiths in a way that a Muslim or Jew could not have?

Do you think there is a reason why it's hard to convince the alien that Christianity is the real, right faith?

Pastor Lucky's Magic Cure All

Imagine your brother gets cancer. What he needs is proper treatment, but he has pinned his hopes on an unproven product which he thinks will stop its spread and control the pain—an all-in-one solution that *just works*.

You're suspicious since there's no supporting science. Your brother has unwavering confidence, and he tells you about how great it is and how amazing the inventor must be. You investigate.

You track it down to a traveling carnival where you find a woman who tells you that the now-deceased inventor was a guy calling himself Pastor Lucky. He wasn't really a pastor or knowledgeable about medicine. She says he was a very kind and charismatic person who convinced himself and those around him that the potion he made could cure people's ailments. This woman even tells you her mother was one of his followers who told everyone she knew how miraculous it was and how amazing Pastor Lucky was.

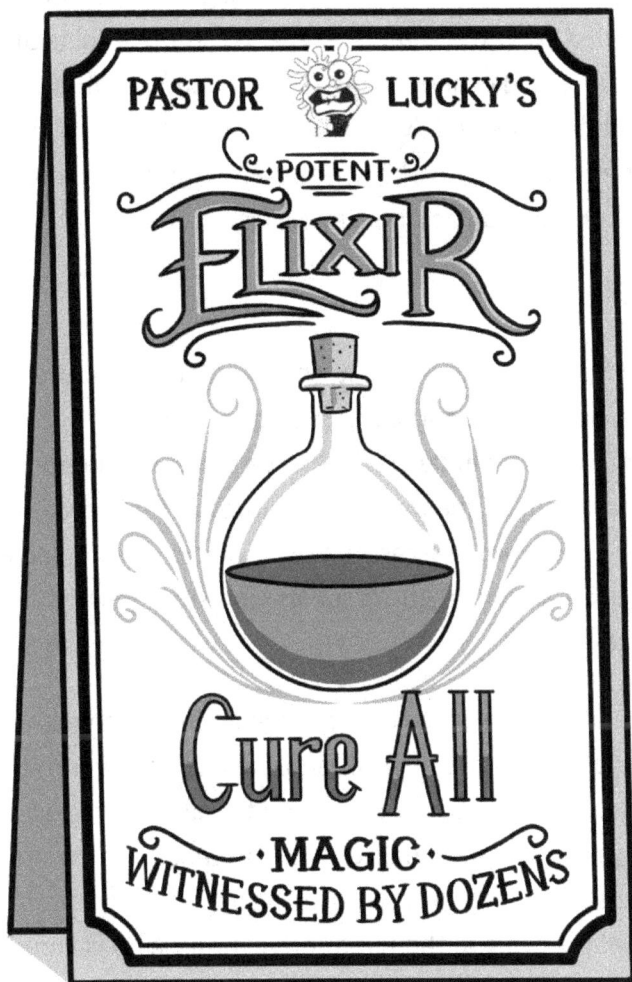

It becomes painfully clear to you how this "magic elixir" got its reputation: it was the brainchild of a very persuasive, committed, and alluring individual. People around him became devoted followers, got taken with him, helped grow the legend, exaggerated the effects of its powers, and sold others on his abilities and his potion until they both became widely known. The man, the story, and the hope took on a life of their own and that is all there really is, or was, to Pastor Lucky's Magic Cure All.

Questions

This story, and real ones like it, show the pattern those legends, myths, and miracle stories often follow: a charismatic leader in desperate times provides a hope story that can heal the pain using impressionable recruits to spread the word and testify to its powers. Are you able to see just how closely the Jesus-as-God story fits this template?

The lore of a divine Jesus took hold in a time when many answers about nature, physics and the universe weren't available. So, it was easier back then to talk of miracles, sorcery, and gods as actual solutions to those unanswered questions. Would it surprise you to learn that there were many people living in the twentieth century who claimed to be divine prophets, performed miracles, and had many followers?[42]

Welcome to God Land

Until you turned seven, you had no exposure to God or faith, at which time you fell into a ten-year coma. At the facility you awake in, you meet someone who catches you up about things, including spirituality.

He talks about it in the abstract only, nothing about the particular faiths. Soon, you form a sense that, yes, there is a creator, that life doesn't appear random, that there must be an intention or meaning imparted to the world, and that this creator seems to have made all this with you in mind. So, you have a basic, generic sense of faith in a personal god.

Your thoughtful friend realizes that depending on where in the world you had woken up—the United States, Israel, Afghanistan, Eastern India—there would be a bias toward the dominant faith of that region, a condition which of course has no bearing on which god created the universe. He wants to preserve as best he can your pristine perspective so that it's you, not your setting, that guides your faith journey.

The next talk with your friend will be your introduction to the existing faiths of the world. Essentially, you'll be where the person is in this picture: having a newfound godly faith but being a clean slate in terms of which is the right faith to commit to.

Questions

Assume you were this young man with this newfound generic sense about god. What guidance does the Christian God provide that anyone could understand to help eliminate the non-Christian faiths from your options?

Several weeks into your search, your health declines. A Hindu family who cares for you well and prays frequently for your condition to improve takes you in. You get better and it appears that this happens in response to the family's prayers. If you choose Hinduism as your faith, did you make the right choice?

Burning Desire Problem

Read this passage from the Bible about someone who would like God's help to win a battle:

> 30 And Jephthah made a vow to the Lord: "If you give the Ammonites into my hands, 31 whatever comes out of the door of my house to meet me when I return in triumph from the Ammonites will be the Lord's, and I will sacrifice it as a burnt offering."

> 32 Then Jephthah went over to fight the Ammonites, and the Lord gave them into his hands. 33 He devastated twenty towns from Aroer to the vicinity of Minnith, as far as Abel Keramim. Thus Israel subdued Ammon. 34 When Jephthah returned to his home in Mizpah, who should come out to meet him but his daughter, dancing to the sound of timbrels! She was an only child.

Except for her he had neither son nor daughter. 35 When he saw her, he tore his clothes and cried, "Oh no, my daughter! You have brought me down and I am devastated. I have made a vow to the Lord that I cannot break." 36 "My father," she replied, "you have given your word to the Lord. Do to me just as you promised, now that the Lord has avenged you of your enemies, the Ammonites. 37 But grant me this one request," she said. "Give me two months to roam the hills and weep with my friends, because I will never marry." 38 "You may go," he said. And he let her go for two months. She and her friends went into the hills and wept because she would never marry. 39 After the two months, she returned to her father, and he did to her as he had vowed. And she was a virgin.

Judges 11:30–39[43]

Questions

There are some good values here that God wants to illustrate—love and devotion. Do you see anything in this passage, however, that might seem to endorse cruel, rash, or morally questionable behavior?

God chose this man over others to make the points in his story. Do you feel good about a person who promises to kill someone at random in order to have his prayers answered?

Let's give Jephthah the benefit of the doubt and say this was just the way some erratic people behaved back then. Let's also give God a pass and say that he was making a lesson out of Jephthah's recklessness as to the importance of keeping promises. Still, you read God accepted Jephthah's offer to murder someone for his help in winning a battle. He didn't have to. He could have said no one should kill indiscriminately to win God's favor. If you didn't know this story came from the Bible, would you embrace it as moral?

The Christian Levels

There is a lot of back and forth about how Christians should interpret the Bible. Nevertheless, there is clear guidance in the Bible about reading it literally, which begs the questions: what is Christianity and what makes a real Christian? Is everyone who says they're Christian a Christian? Is believing in Jesus enough?

If embracing the Son of God were enough, there wouldn't be other warnings that fill the Bible. It obviously takes more than that to be a bona fide Christian. You could argue that only literalists are the real Christians. But a more tolerant view sorts Christians by the degree to which they reinterpret key aspects of the Bible. Below, you'll see a *Scale of Christian Committedness* with believers falling into one of five categories.

Review the levels and the descriptions to see which one describes you best.

Level 1 - The True Believers

Along with its charming stories, the Bible includes shocking cruelty and unlikely explanations—and the true believers accept every word as unimpeachable gospel. It's not pretty, but if you want to be unquestionably Christian, this is the camp for you.

EVERY WORD,
JUST AS IT IS
WRITTEN

Level 2 - Out with the Old, In with the New Crowd

You may be fully devoted to Jesus, but you can't accept a God who lacks basic insights and has a host of deplorable tendencies. Level 2 Christians are extreme, but have their limits.

NOT THAT OLD
TESTAMENT
BUT THE NEW ONE
FOR SURE

Level 3 - Take-What-You-Want Gang

This is the most popular level, but it's not just one interpretation. Rather, it is a million different approaches, an attitude that lets everyone have their own viewpoint while feeling as though they're members of the same social group.

LIKE MOST PEOPLE,
I INTERPRET THE BIBLE
IN ORDER
TO UNDERSTAND
IT'S CONTEXT
AND MEANING

Level 4 - Core Beliefs Optional

There are Christ-leaning folks who have trouble with the idea that there's absolutely no way to God but through the Son; they aren't sure it's wrong, but they're willing to believe there may be other valid paths to salvation. If you're trying to be Christian, or accept it as one of the right faiths, then you align with the Core Beliefs Optional group.

GOOD,
GOD-LOVING PEOPLE
OF OTHER FAITHS
HAVE A SHOT
AT HEAVEN

Level 5 - Anything Godly Goes

Level 5 Christians are just flirting with faith. Their idea of spirituality means that if your actions match your beliefs, then this is your connection with God.

AS LONG AS YOU'RE TRUE TO YOUR FAITH, GOD IS ALRIGHT WITH THAT

Questions

Which is your level of Christianity on this scale: 1, 2, 3, 4, or 5?

If you're not a Level 1 Christian, answering this question may bother you. Maybe you feel no one has the right to rank how "Christian" you are and tell you that you're less faithful than another. Still, after reading 2 Peter 1:20,[44] are you able to square that with your refusal to accept *everything* in the Bible?

Why does a "Level 3 Christian" believe he's a Christian even if he rejects much of what the faith requires?

A Tough Choice

Think about a father who intends to exhibit tough love to his son through the following trial. The father expects the young man to select the dog that is the best companion, the right companion—in the father's opinion. You can assume there's nothing obvious that would or should bias the boy toward any specific dog, other than the fact that one breed is slightly more common in their location. In other words, any of the dogs could be suitable companions to him.

Four advocates bring their dogs to the boy's home. The advocates will try to compel the boy to choose their dog. The advocates have brought written booklets to sum up the case to urge the boy to select that dog and remind him of some dire consequences for selecting the wrong one.

For selecting the companion the father believes is correct, the boy will receive a great and expensive gift of his choosing. For guessing wrong, the family will disown the boy and they won't allow him to return home. To make the challenge more difficult, the boy is told the dogs at hand are simply the most likely companions to choose from. Any of many other breeds could end up being the father's selection—the "right" answer. In addition, choosing no dog—that is, no companion—could be the choice the father expects the boy to make.

The father appears to be indifferent to how impossibly difficult this challenge is for the boy. He says this is a test of intuition. There's no practice challenge. There's no second chance.

Questions

To avoid being disowned, the boy must select the dog the father has in mind. Given what's at stake, is it incumbent on the father to have provided a clear criterion for selecting the right dog?

Let's give the father a pass about the test itself and say this could be a useful exercise for developing intuitive decision-making skills under pressure. The matter, then, is whether the consequences are too harsh. Is there a point at which *tough love* becomes so tough as to be un-loving?

Surely, you see the "right" dog riddle and the stiff penalties as a way of illustrating your trial to guess the "right" God to worship and the punishment that could await you for a wrong choice. If you think the father's actions are abusive, but your feelings about the Christian God remain warm, why do you think that is?

Slavery Problem

Read these words from the Holy Bible:

God said:

> When a man strikes his slave, male or
> female, with a rod, and he dies there and
> then, he must be avenged. But if he survives
> a day or two, he is not to be avenged, since
> he is the other's property. Exodus 21:2–
> 11.[45]

God said:

> When a man sells his daughter as a slave,
> she will not be freed at the end of six years
> as the men are. Exodus 21:7.[45]

God said:

> Servants, be obedient to them that are your
> masters according to the flesh, with fear
> and trembling, in singleness of your heart,
> as unto Christ Ephesians 6:5.[46]

Questions

If God wants those who came after ancient times to know his objection to owning and beating people, do you think a Bible with verses like these is a good way to communicate that?

Would a morally supreme being with the benefit of modern-day knowledge say that beating a slave within a day of her life is okay (not punishable) since she is someone's property?

Imagine for a moment that you didn't know about Christianity yet. Someone explains to you, before taking you to a church service, that being a Christian would entail worshiping this God, doing what he commands, no matter what, and dedicating your life to him. In fact, your friend tells you that you already have no choice in one important way. If you fail to respond to his command, God will send you to a much worse place. Would it occur to you that this sounds a lot like a forced slavery arrangement?

Found the True Faith

Think about your priest or pastor who has inspired you with their faith. You are both Christians, but this individual is more devout than you, prays more, knows more about the Bible, and is more giving than you. He walks the walk. His life revolves around his Christian faith.

He is your Christian role model until one day when he tells you he has found a new faith—Islam. He has already converted, and he is so happy that he found "the true faith." He explains that when he prays now, he hears God's voice with a clarity he never knew was possible. He shares other reasons Islam is better than Christianity and why Christianity is misguided.

He says you will be so much happier as a Muslim and he will guide you the way he did when he was lost—as a Christian.

Questions

You have trusted this man with your innermost thoughts and issues. He has never let you down, not once. Deep down, you trust him more than you do your spouse. Following his advice over the years has been among the smartest things you have done. If he is that reliable and that good for you and your family, would you consider following his advice this time?

Since it's God's love for you that keeps you from impulsively switching faiths, do you expect some definitive guidance from God—perhaps something you can distinguish from your own reasoning?

Omniscient Moral Leader

Infinite awareness, understanding and insight—that is omniscience. Just the idea of it is mind blowing.

Think of the amazing things an omniscient being can conceive. For example, how God invented atoms and how they can transform into energy and back.

$$E = mc^2$$

$$E^2 = (pc)^2 + (mc^2)^2$$

$$S = \frac{c^3 KA}{4hG}$$

$$s = ut + \tfrac{1}{2}at^2$$

Then there is you, able to read this book, having a rich and complex life, having grown from a clump of cells which came from the dust of a star that exploded long ago, which scientists can trace back to whatever the beginning was. God started with a point of energy long ago and knew the path of a few of those eventual particles which would ultimately result in you. One tiny mistake along the way means you wouldn't be here. Just think of what an omniscient being could understand.

God's physics achievements are impressive, but his primary job is not that of a cosmic inventor. He is the judge of your soul and everyone else's, right? It's great that he can make stars across eons of time, but what does it matter if revelation and spiritual consequences are unfair to you? The risk of everlasting torture you never agreed to is a big deal and arguably should get at least as much attention to detail as the other stuff.

Expectations are high for a well thought out and fair system of soul adjudication.

Instead of marveling at $E=MC^2$, let's be in awe of a few profound rules of God's revelation and morality, or at least ones we'd expect the inventor of space-time to enact:

Let's envision:

𝕿𝖍𝖊 𝕾𝖎𝖝 𝕻𝖗𝖔𝖒𝖎𝖘𝖊𝖘
of God's Revelation and Morality

1. I will write the official book of revelation myself and deliver it directly into the hands of any human who wants it in order to avoid confusion and errors that might arise through outsourcing the job.

2. I will give humanity effective ways of knowing the Bible is the only divine revelation, so people don't follow the wrong guidance.

3. Given that the Bible includes guidelines of morality, I must demonstrate my condemnation of murder and slavery by not performing or rewarding such behaviors.

4. Having seen the future of the universe before creating it, it's clear that condemning non-believers to eternal torture isn't an optimal deterrent or a sensible solution—so I won't do that.

5. If I decide not to clarify that I am the one, true God who must be worshiped and glorified and people worship and glorify other gods, or no god at all, then there will be no punishment for this.

6. I expect people to be as kind and responsible as they can be, given that the traits they have are the ones that I gave them.

Questions

For each statement above, decide whether it should be and is a basic principle of God's Revelation and morality guidelines.

Compare The Six Promises with the Ten Commandments in Exodus 20:2–17.[47] When you consider the apparent forethought and brilliance given to designing the space-time continuum, don't you think God gave too little effort to matters of moral importance like you find in Exodus and elsewhere in the Bible?

Does it seem reasonable that the Christian God could design the entire universe but cannot give a Christian and a Muslim a way to agree which god they should worship?

Faith Festival

One by one, of each faith and the parts listed, say out loud the name, like this:

<u>Christianity</u> - <u>holy book,</u> <u>afterlife,</u> <u>miracle stories,</u> <u>rituals & props</u>

Say only the faith name and the double underlined parts. Try not to stop until you get through them all. Be sure to glance at the differences between the faiths as you go. The exercise will take around one minute.

Test questions are at the bottom.

Start here:

Zoroastrianism

God & prophets Ahura Mazda, Zoroaster

Big influence on Christianity & Judaism

God is an all-knowing, all-powerful creator of the universe

Holy Book Zend-Avesta

Afterlife House of Songs, Daena & Angra Mainyu

Miracle stories Parting the water of a river

Rituals & props Kusti

Worshipers in history Millions[48]

Islam

God & prophets Allah, Muhammad

God is an all-knowing, all-powerful creator of the universe

Holy book Quran

Afterlife Akhirah, Iblis & Mashallah

Miracle stories Muhammad split the moon in two

Rituals & props Ramadan, Hajj pilgrimage, Taqiyah

Worshipers in history Billions [49]

Ancient Egyptian Religion

God & prophets Isis, Osiris

Gods are life giving creators of the universe

Holy book Pyramid Texts

Afterlife Duat, Akh & Apophis

Miracle stories Heka magic events

Rituals & props Maat, divine order works

Worshipers in history Millions [50]

Hinduism

God & prophets Vishnu, Brahma, Shiva

God is part of everything in the universe

Holy book The Vedas

Afterlife Reincarnation, Karma

Miracle stories Beheaded man revived with an elephant's head

Rituals & props Purusharthas, Marga, Yoga

Worshipers in history Billions [51]

Baha'i

God & prophets Baha'u'llah, others

God is an all-knowing, all-powerful creator of the universe

Holy book The Kitab-i-Aqdas

Afterlife Soul lives on in eternal realm

Miracle stories Cured infertility, Haifa takeover prediction

Rituals & props Nineteen day feast, Funeral prayer recitation

Worshipers in history Millions [52]

Buddhism

God & prophets Siddhartha

God is everywhere in the universe

Holy book Tripitaka

Afterlife Reincarnation, enlightenment

Miracle stories Still Shadow, Floating Hairknot

Rituals & props Nirvana, Mahayana

Worshipers in history Billions [53]

Tengriism

God & prophets Tengri, the sky god

God is part of everything in the universe

Holy book Orkhon Inscriptions

Afterlife Erlik, Tengri

Miracle stories Spirits speak to select individuals

Rituals & props Mudang, Belukha

Worshipers in history Millions [54]

Christianity

God & prophets The Trinity, Jesus, Ezekiel

God is an all-knowing, all-powerful creator of the universe

Holy book The Bible

Afterlife Heaven, hell

Miracle stories Multiplying fish, curing the sick, virgin birth

Rituals & props Christmas, Baptism

Worshipers in history Billions [55]

Aztec

God & prophets Tonatiuh, Tlaloc

God is a powerful creator who made the sun and moon

Holy book Codex Borbonicus

Afterlife Tlaloc's paradise

Miracle stories Quetzalcoatl acts

Rituals & props Sacrifice to Tonatiuh, Ceremonial priests

Worshipers in history Millions [56]

Judaism

God & prophets Abraham, Moses

God is an all-knowing, all-powerful creator of the universe

Holy book Tanakh, Talmud

Afterlife Heaven, hell

Miracle stories Bush burned but not consumed, Red Sea split

Rituals & props Hanukkah, Bar-Mitzvah, Yarmulkes

Worshipers in history Millions [57]

Wicca

God & prophets Horned god, Oak King

God is part of everything in the universe

Holy book Book of Shadows

Afterlife Summerland

Miracle stories Healing spells, mental health spells

Rituals & props Initiation rebirth, Witch bottle

Worshipers in history Millions [58]

Shintoism

God & prophets Amida, Hachiman

Supernatural Ideas Way of the Spirits

Holy book The Kojiki

Afterlife Pure Land, Kegare & Makoto

Miracle stories Kannushi

Rituals & props Kamidana worship shrines

Worshipers in history Millions [59]

Norse Paganism

God & prophets Ymir, Odin, Thor

Gods are powerful creators and controllers of the world

Holy book Edda Elda

Afterlife Niflheim, Valhalla

Miracle stories The Seiðr, future seeing by Völva Spakona

Rituals & props Animal sacrifices, the Mjolnir hammer

Worshipers in history Millions [60]

Questions

Do you get the feeling that people need the same basic parts of a faith story, regardless of the place, the time, or the featured god?

If you had not come to this exercise with your Christian faith, would you see much about it that stands out from other faiths?

What is it about Christianity that makes it stand out from the other faiths? Why couldn't you explain this to a devoted Muslim to convince him?

A Problem in Heaven

Consider the scenario in which you revel in your marriage and are very much in love with your wife. Sadly, your heart suddenly gives out and you pass away. You awaken in heaven, glad you're there, but missing your wife who will surely join you one day. To your surprise, you discover your wife wasn't faithful to you while you were alive and has no interest in seeing you in heaven, even if God accepted her. You are left to ponder this.

Questions

If it is as easy as this to envision an unpleasant heaven experience, do you think there might be a problem with your ideas about heaven?

After your death, would you want to be in the dead man's place, being in *heaven* but aware that the love of your life doesn't care to be with you in the afterlife?

Imagine you are allowed into heaven, but your children are suffering in hell. Being the selfless, loving person you are, you ask God to take them in place of you. He refuses. What kind of heaven experience will you have?

The Better Bible Problem

The Bible is the best, clearest book possible, the one whose context transcends the ages, the great Revelation, the one produced by a supreme being with incredible insights of morality we never could have imagined.

God's book is the only one ever produced by a supreme being. Because of this, it cannot be improved on—at least not by a human being.

But is it unimprovable? Could we make the Bible clearer? Could we get behavioral guidance without the poor values some of those stories contain? Could we rewrite the Bible so it works just as well in other times as it did in the first century, without people having to guess what it means? *Maybe at some point we could go even deeper to produce a document worthy of a supreme being and his one and only attempt at revealing himself to his people.* For now, let's find one example and see what we can do.

Original Verse

> *But if the thing is true, and evidences of virginity are not found for the young woman, then they shall bring out the young woman to the door of her father's house, and the men of her city shall stone her to death with stones, because she has done a disgraceful thing in Israel, to play the harlot in her father's house. So you shall put away the evil from among you.*

> Deuteronomy 22:20–21[61]

Can we make it better? Let's talk it out first:

There are some problems here we should deal with:

1. This God-endorsed plan indicates that in response to rumors, grown men should force a young girl to get naked as they inspect her vagina's inner anatomy.

2. It's common knowledge now that hymen breakage, which is what the men were looking for, can and does happen for reasons that have nothing to do with sex.

3. Even assuming the girl had sex just before or at the beginning of the marriage, there are other situations that could have happened: her fiancé could have beaten and raped her, she may have mental health issues, or perhaps her fiancé/new husband cheated on her. These are important things to consider before killing a teenage girl.

4. Regardless of why a fifteen-year-old girl forced to marry someone who might have sex with someone else, the punishment God appears to endorse is torture and death, which may have been standard in the first century, but is clearly not a proportional reaction to her "wrongdoing."

We can make this better

Improved Verse

> *If the male betrothed, or his father, believes or is informed that the young woman has failed to remain faithful in the marriage, then the men of the village shall gather and see that the matter is closed to them. If the family of the male betrothed believes the dowry is insufficient considering the accusation, then the marriage shall be forthwith dissolved, and the dowry returned to the young woman's family.*

> *Pastor Lucky's New & Improved Bible*

It's not perfect, but by first century standards, it's far more civilized than "God and Lot's" approach.

Questions

Should it be this easy to improve the Bible?

If it's as easy as this to improve the Bible, it should already be that good, right?

Do you think it says something about the divine nature of the Bible, given that anyone can make it clearer and less immoral while improving the message?

Punishment Problem

God punishes the unredeemed sinners and those who have not accepted Jesus as their savior harshly. But why? God is clever. One would expect an impressive strategy behind his actions to help convince those who struggle to get onboard and provide them with the motivation to follow through. And even if God deemed a punishment appropriate, it should be in proportion to the sin. So how would this work?[62]

What if it were for deterrence? A deterrent is intended to reduce the chance that a behavior happens. It can target an individual or a population. Since no one ever gets to see whether God rejected a person from heaven or showed mercy on them for their beliefs, then the deterrent effect of this threat would be ineffective and not a good incentive.

What if it were for incapacitation? This is preventing a behavior by removing someone's ability to do it. This would be like God removing you from the streets for not believing in him so others won't get the idea. Again, after death, there's no point in incapacitating someone for this "wrongdoing." Death already takes care of that. The damage was done.

What if it were to rehabilitate wrongdoers? This would be to prevent future wrongdoing by putting someone on the right path. Again, the sentence to hell is permanent. People could not show it rehabilitated their godly belief before God.

Maybe it's for retribution. This is getting even, inflicting pain. If the Bible is true, then this is the domain of this punishment. God is taking revenge on you for not believing in him.

Then there's *restitution*, paying back what you stole. This would be you somehow working off the unacceptable behavior of not believing in Jesus or behaving right. Again, this would not be possible as the sentence to hell is irrevocable and there's nothing the sentenced person can do to change that.

There is a possible purpose for the punishment of banishment to hell: God hurts you in response to you believing in the wrong religion. Anything is possible with God, right? The question here is: is it reasonable? Is it reasonable to think the supreme being of the universe is going to inflict pain and torture on non-believers with no hope for any of this to make any difference to the accused or to anyone else? Does this sound like an effective, well-conceived plan for how to deal with those souls? It's not reasonable. It's not a good or mature plan. As shown above, it's a poor and ineffective strategy for encouraging people to believe in Jesus and Christianity.

Questions

Now that you know the various reasons for specific punishments, does the Bible's punishment seem well-thought out to you?

In place of punishments, could God have implemented a better system for encouraging humans to get behind the plans he has for them?

That's What the Muslim Said

Think about the lives of two families of two faiths living in two parts of the world: a Christian and a Muslim family. These are all good people who are thrust into the same situation: each family's son becomes gravely ill. Needing their faith and their god, they each pray for their child to improve, which doctors tell them isn't likely. Fortunately for both families, the boys' sickness disappears at a miraculous rate. From the standpoint of each family, it is as though praying was like pressing a "be cured" button.

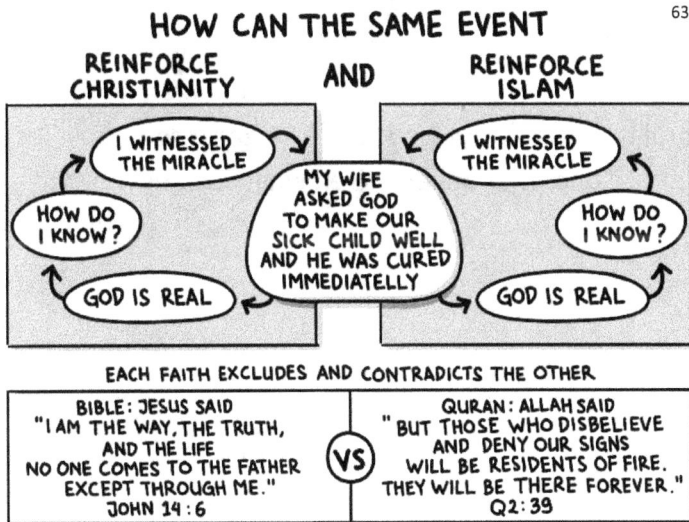

HOW CAN THE SAME EVENT [63, 64]

REINFORCE CHRISTIANITY **AND** REINFORCE ISLAM

I WITNESSED THE MIRACLE

HOW DO I KNOW?

GOD IS REAL

MY WIFE ASKED GOD TO MAKE OUR SICK CHILD WELL AND HE WAS CURED IMMEDIATELLY

I WITNESSED THE MIRACLE

HOW DO I KNOW?

GOD IS REAL

EACH FAITH EXCLUDES AND CONTRADICTS THE OTHER

BIBLE: JESUS SAID	VS	QURAN: ALLAH SAID
"I AM THE WAY, THE TRUTH, AND THE LIFE NO ONE COMES TO THE FATHER EXCEPT THROUGH ME." JOHN 14:6		"BUT THOSE WHO DISBELIEVE AND DENY OUR SIGNS WILL BE RESIDENTS OF FIRE. THEY WILL BE THERE FOREVER." Q2:39

Each family is relieved that they hold the faith and religion they do. If they didn't, they assume God would not have heard their prayers. They are comforted that they are on the right side of their faith's exclusivity, as stated in their holy books.

Questions

Did God answer the prayer of the Muslim family's wife in this case?

If the Muslim family is wrong about their faith, then the child's improvement was just their good fortune. God must know that this devout but misguided family will interpret the child's improvement as a response to their prayer. Clearly, this misunderstanding will only reinforce their belief in the wrong God. In your understanding of morality, is it right for God to hold them accountable for their blasphemous beliefs, given what you know here?

He Makes the World a Better Place

Think about an adult, Sam, a nice Jewish guy who works hard, takes up the slack for others who struggle, and gives to the needy. He's God-loving and lives a virtuous life, but isn't pious. The world is better with this kind of person in it.

Sadly, he dies on the way home one day. He expects to wake in Heaven but finds himself on the way to the other place. During his descent, he asks God why. Sam says, "Look at the life I lived! I worshiped the God I thought existed. I did as I thought I was right. Why would you want to banish me for this? I did not know I was doing anything wrong. I would have changed my ways if I had known."

Questions

Do you think it's a good thing that God treats Sam this way?

If you had to choose, which world would you rather live in: one with lots of Sams in it? Or one filled with, for example, abusive but apologetic Jesus lovers?

If Sam is a good person and follows the faith he believes to be valid, do you understand the point of God banishing him from heaven?

Final Thoughts About the Refusal

Imagine that archeologists find an ancient copy of the Bible. Biblical scholars unanimously agree on its authenticity and they think it's the first copy made from the original Bible as we know it today. The scholars noticed something interesting though: two pages of it were bound together and between them is never-before-seen scripture. They will read aloud the words but beforehand, you ponder the significance of what you might learn.

Questions

Are there words you could hear that would cause you to doubt God's love?

Is your mind open to learning something new about Christianity, *including words from the Bible itself*?

What if the words were something objectionable: would you refuse to believe them unless they comport with what you already believe and cherish about the faith?

Consider Leaving a Review

Thank you so much for reading *Enemy Playbook*. If you have a moment, please consider providing a review of the book on Amazon so others may have a chance of finding it. Thanks again.

-Pastor Lucky

www.amazon.com

Sign Up for My Newsletter

If you would like to know more about new books, new products, content updates, or what Pastor Lucky is up to, please visit the website to sign up for the newsletter.

www.pastorlucky.com

References

1. Hamilton C. The theodicy of the "good anthropocene." *Environ humanit*. 2016;7(1):233-238.

2. Green A. Joseph Ibn Kaspi on contradictions in the bible. *J Relig*. 2022;102(2):184-203.

3. Competing Claims for Truth. Accessed June 8, 2022. https://www.bc.edu/content/dam/files/research_sites/cjl/texts/cjrelations/resources/articles/lasker.htm

4. Matthew 13. Accessed June 8, 2022. https://www.bible.com/bible/59/MAT.13.ESV

5. Review of Bostrom's Simulation Argument. Accessed June 8, 2022. https://web.stanford.edu/class/symbsys205/BostromReview.html

6. NFL fines Belichick, strips Patriots of draft pick. Published September 13, 2007. Accessed June 8, 2022. https://www.patriots.com/news/nfl-fines-belichick-strips-patriots-of-draft-pick-101526

7. Vanderpool K. The Age of Deconstruction and Future of the Church. RELEVANT. Published April 7, 2021. Accessed June 8, 2022. https://relevantmagazine.com/faith/the-age-of-deconstruction-and-future-of-the-church/

8. Celine. Differences Between Belief and Knowledge. Published April 17, 2013. Accessed June 8, 2022. http://www.differencebetween.net/language/words-language/differences-between-belief-and-knowledge/

9. Garrett N, González-Garzón AM, Foulkes L, Levita L, Sharot T.

Updating Beliefs under Perceived Threat. *J Neurosci*. 2018;38(36):7901-7911.

10. Cochrane A, Barnes-Holmes D, Barnes-Holmes Y. The Perceived-Threat Behavioral Approach Test (PT-BAT): Measuring Avoidance in High-, Mid-, and Low-Spider-Fearful Participants. *Psychol Rec*. 2017;58(4):585-596.

11. Barlow DH, Craske MG, Cerny JA, Klosko JS. Behavioral treatment of panic disorder. *Behav Ther*. 1989;20(2):261-282.

12. The role of maladaptive beliefs in cognitive-behavioral therapy: Evidence from social anxiety disorder. *Behav Res Ther*. 2012;50(5):287-291.

13. Phobias. Accessed June 8, 2022. https://www.hopkinsmedicine.org/health/conditions-and-diseases/phobias

14. What is "Compartmentalization" with regard to religion? Accessed June 8, 2022. https://agnostic.com/discussion/198490/what-is-compartmentalization-with-regard-to-religion

15. Sylvester J. Christianity: Fundamentally Illogical. Atheist Alliance International. Published January 17, 2022. Accessed June 8, 2022. https://www.atheistalliance.org/blog/christianity-fundamentally-illogical/

16. Risen JL. Believing what we do not believe: Acquiescence to superstitious beliefs and other powerful intuitions. *Psychol Rev*. 2016;123(2):182-207.

17. Heywood BT, Bering JM. "Meant to be": how religious beliefs and cultural religiosity affect the implicit bias to think teleologically. *Religion Brain Behav*. 2014;4(3):183-201.

18. Kruger J, Wirtz D, Miller DT. Counterfactual thinking and the first instinct fallacy. Published online 2005. Accessed July 5, 2022. https://www.ncbi.nlm.nih.gov/pubmed/15898871

19. Mughal S, Azhar Y, Mahon MM, Siddiqui WJ. Grief Reaction. In: *StatPearls [Internet]*. StatPearls Publishing; 2022.

20. APA Dictionary of Psychology. Accessed June 8, 2022. https://dictionary.apa.org/

21. circular argument. Encyclopedia Britannica. Accessed June 8, 2022. https://www.britannica.com/topic/circular-argument

22. A Christian Cannot Recognize Muhammad as a Prophet. Reformed Free Publishing Association. Accessed June 8, 2022. https://rfpa.org/blogs/news/84803716-no-a-christian-cannot-recognize-muhammad-as-a-prophet

23. Misselbrook D. The Euthyphro dilemma. *Br J Gen Pract*. 2013;63(610):263-263.

24. O'Reilly BD. When You Say You Believe In God, What Do You Mean? Accessed June 8, 2022. https://pew.org/2Tv2Z6R

25. Chonyi T. Buddha's Miracles manifest - sravasti abbey - A Buddhist monastery. Sravasti Abbey. Published February 10, 2021. Accessed July 31, 2022. https://sravastiabbey.org/buddhas-miracles-manifest/

26. Nursi BS. Eighth Sign: It explains the miracle of the Prophet (pbuh) about water gushing forth from his hands like a faucet and the increase in water when his mouth water contacts it. Questions on Islam. Accessed July 31, 2022. https://questionsonislam.com/article/eighth-sign-it-explains-miracle-prophet-pbuh-about-water-gushing-forth-his-hands-faucet-and

27.   Cherry K. Why Do We Favor Information That Confirms Our Existing Beliefs? Verywell Mind. Published March 7, 2014. Accessed June 8, 2022. https://www.verywellmind.com/what-is-a-confirmation-bias-2795024

28.   Forrest P. The Epistemology of Religion. Published online April 23, 1997. Accessed June 8, 2022. https://plato.stanford.edu/entries/religion-epistemology/#:~:text=Evidentialism%20implies%20that%20full%20religious,that%20there%20is%20a%20God.

29.   Wikipedia contributors. Discourse on the Method. Wikipedia, The Free Encyclopedia. Published July 22, 2022. https://en.wikipedia.org/w/index.php?title=Discourse_on_the_Method&oldid=1099722139

30.   HOW TO DEBATE. Accessed June 8, 2022. https://www.sfu.ca/cmns/130d1/HOWTODEBATE.htm

31.   Presuppositional apologetics. Published June 4, 2004. Accessed June 20, 2022. https://en.wikipedia.org/wiki/Presuppositional_apologetics

32.   Craig WL. In Defense of the Kalam Cosmological Argument. *Faith Philos*. 1997;14(2):236-247.

33.   Gould SJ. Nonoverlapping Magisteria. *Filozoficzne Aspekty Genezy*. 2014;(11):7-21.

34.   *Sam Harris: Playing Tennis without A Net*.; 2013. Accessed July 31, 2022. https://youtu.be/1q-387Zb54Q

35.   Stephens M. Thinking as Christian virtue: Reason and persuasion for a fractious age. In: *Innovating Christian Education Research*. Springer Nature Singapore; 2021:31-44.

36.   Response to restrictive policies: Reconciling system justification

and psychological reactance. *Organ Behav Hum Decis Process*. 2013;122(2):152-162.

37.   Genesis 1. Accessed June 8, 2022. https://www.bible.com/bible/59/GEN.1.ESV

38.   Matthew 19:24 Again I tell you, it is easier for a camel to go through the eye of a needle than for a rich person to enter the kingdom of God.". Accessed July 27, 2022. https://www.bible.com/bible/59/MAT.19.24.ESV

39.   Koukl G. *Tactics: A Game Plan for Discussing Your Christian Convictions*. Zondervan; 2009.

40.   Trevors GJ, Muis KR, Pekrun R, Sinatra GM, Winne PH. Identity and epistemic emotions during knowledge revision: A potential account for the backfire effect. *Discourse Process*. 2016;53(5-6):339-370.

41.   Revelation 19. Accessed June 8, 2022. https://www.bible.com/bible/59/REV.19.ESV

42.   Sutton C. Seven men around the world who each claim to be Jesus Christ. NZ Herald. Published December 24, 2017. Accessed June 20, 2022. https://www.nzherald.co.nz/world/seven-men-around-the-world-who-each-claim-to-be-jesus-christ/2W27IHL7PIQLTO5SFAPPAMN5HM/

43.   Judges 11. Accessed June 8, 2022. https://www.bible.com/bible/59/JDG.11.ESV

44.   2 Peter 1. Accessed June 8, 2022. https://www.bible.com/bible/59/2PE.1.ESV

45.   Exodus 21. Accessed June 8, 2022. https://www.bible.com/bible/59/EXO.21.ESV

46.   Ephesians 6. Accessed June 8, 2022.
       https://www.bible.com/bible/59/EPH.6.ESV

47.   Exodus 20. Accessed June 8, 2022.
       https://www.bible.com/bible/59/EXO.20.ESV

48.   Mark JJ. Zoroastrianism. *World History Encyclopedia*. Published
       online December 12, 2019. Accessed June 8, 2022.
       https://www.worldhistory.org/zoroastrianism/

49.   Miracles of Prophet Muhammad. Facts about the Muslims & the
       Religion of Islam - Toll-free hotline 1-877-WHY-ISLAM. Published
       March 30, 2015. Accessed June 8, 2022.
       https://www.whyislam.org/on-faith/miracles-of-prophet-
       muhammad/

50.   Religion in the Lives of the Ancient Egyptians. Accessed June 8,
       2022. https://fathom.lib.uchicago.edu/1/777777190168/

51.   Narayanan V. Hinduism. Encyclopedia Britannica. Accessed June
       8, 2022. https://www.britannica.com/topic/Hinduism

52.   Baha'i Faith. Encyclopedia Britannica. Accessed June 8, 2022.
       https://www.britannica.com/topic/Bahai-Faith

53.   Gautama S, Lama D. Buddhism. HISTORY. Published October 12,
       2017. Accessed June 8, 2022.
       https://www.history.com/topics/religion/buddhism

54.   Mongolia D. The Ancient Religion of Tengriism. Discover
       Mongolia Travel. Published January 7, 2019. Accessed June 8,
       2022. https://www.discovermongolia.mn/blogs/the-ancient-
       religion-of-tengriism

55.   Stefon M. Christianity. Encyclopedia Britannica. Accessed June 8,
       2022. https://www.britannica.com/topic/Christianity

56. Aztecs. HISTORY. Published October 27, 2009. Accessed June 8, 2022. https://www.history.com/topics/ancient-americas/aztecs

57. Feldman LH. Judaism. Encyclopedia Britannica. Accessed June 8, 2022. https://www.britannica.com/topic/Judaism

58. [No title]. Accessed June 8, 2022. https://www.defenseculture.mil/Portals/90/Documents/Toolkit/ReligiousAwareness/FACTS-REL-Wicca-20191106.pdf?ver=2020-01-31-142221-557

59. Hirai N. Shinto. Encyclopedia Britannica. Accessed June 8, 2022. https://www.britannica.com/topic/Shinto

60. Old Norse religion. Published April 30, 2004. Accessed June 8, 2022. https://en.wikipedia.org/wiki/Old_Norse_religion

61. Deuteronomy 22. Accessed June 8, 2022. https://www.bible.com/bible/59/DEU.22.ESV

62. General deterrence. Encyclopedia Britannica. Accessed June 20, 2022. https://www.britannica.com/topic/punishment

63. John 14. Accessed June 8, 2022. https://www.bible.com/bible/59/JHN.14.ESV

64. Surah Al-Baqarah - 1-286. Quran.com. Accessed June 8, 2022. https://quran.com/al-baqarah